SOLOS

for the

VIOLIN PLAYER

With Piano Accompaniment

Selected and Edited by

JOSEF GINGOLD

Ed. 2425

G. SCHIRMER, Inc.

DISTRIBUTED BY

HAL•LEONARD®
CORPORATION

7777 W. BLUEMOUND RD. P.O. BOX 13819 MILWAUKEE, WI 53213

CONTENTS

1. Tambourin

JEAN-JOSEPH MONDONVILLE (1711 - 1772)

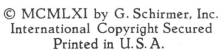

poco largamente

2. The Bells

(1705)

JEAN FERRY REBEL (1661-1747)

Allegro con spirito

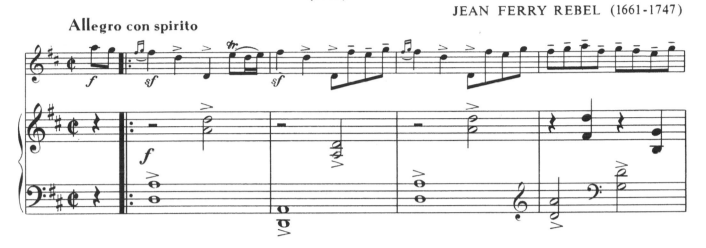

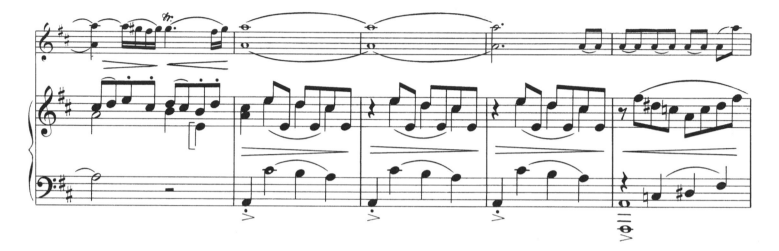

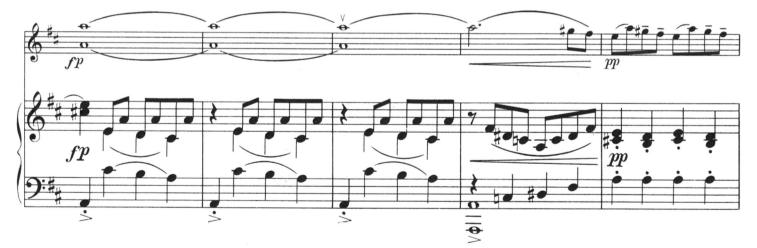

D.C. al Fine

3. Siciliano

from: Sonata 4

JOHANN SEBASTIAN BACH (1685 - 1750)

4. Rondo in D

WOLFGANG AMADEUS MOZART (1756-1791)

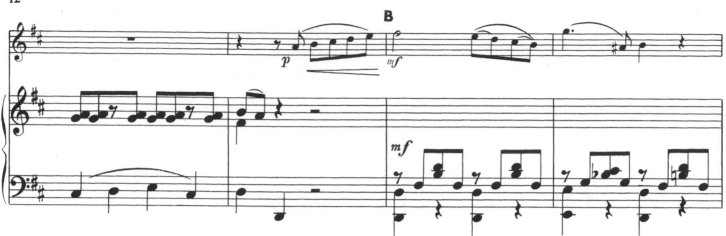

Allegro Spiritoso

JEAN BAPTISTE SENAILLÉ (1687 - 1730)

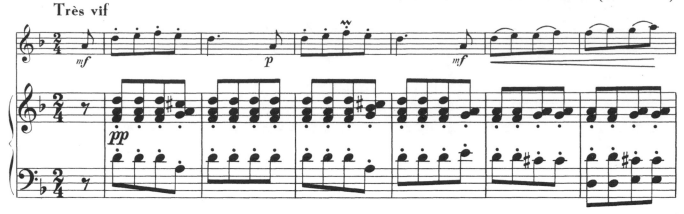

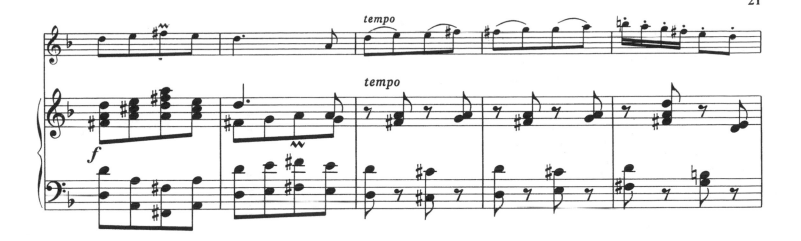

6. Abendlied

(Evening Song)

ROBERT SCHUMANN Op. 85. No. 12
(1810-1856)
arranged by Joseph Joachim

Ausdrucksvoll und sehr gehalten
(**Expressively, very sustained**)

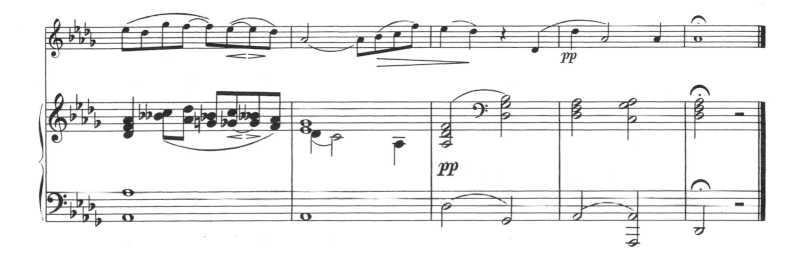

7. Allegro

Excerpt from: Concertpiece

FRANZ SCHUBERT (1797-1828)

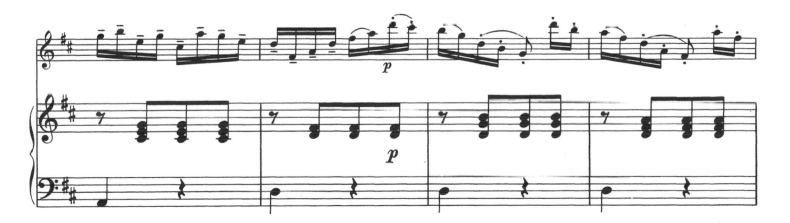

8. Waltz

from: Lyric Pieces, op.12

EDVARD GRIEG (1843-1907)

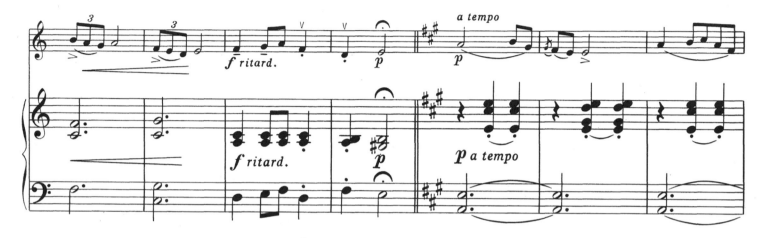

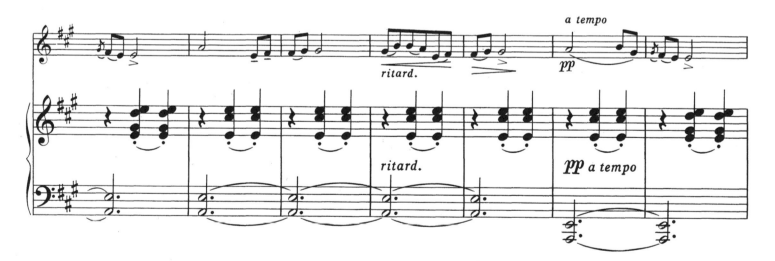

Coda

9. Album Leaf

from: Lyric Pieces, op. 12

EDVARD GRIEG (1843–1907)

10. Sonata No. 12

NICCOLO PAGANINI (1782-1840)

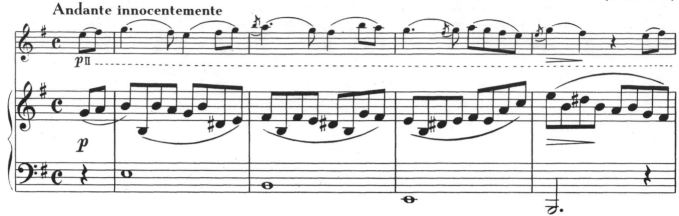

Allegro vivo e spirito

sulla tastiera..

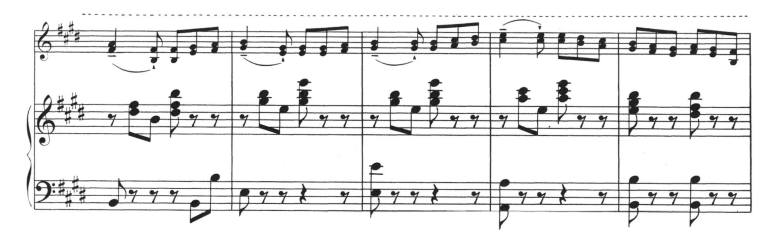

11. Hungarian Dance No. 2

JOHANNES BRAHMS (1833-1897)
arranged by Paul Klengel

Tempo I (Allegro non assai)

12. Adagio

from: Suite in A minor

CHRISTIAN SINDING Op. 10
(1856-1941)

Un poco più mosso

Tempo I

13. Berceuse

GABRIEL FAURÉ Op. 16
(1845-1924)

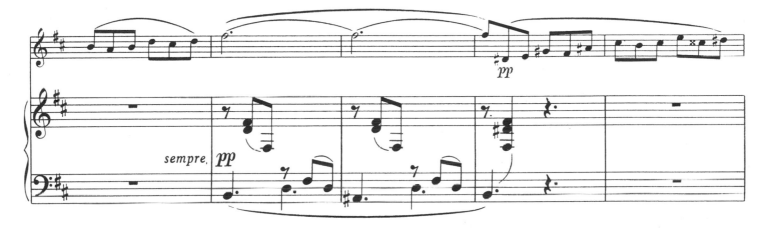

14. Valse Scherzo No. 2

PETER ILYITCH TSCHAIKOWSKY (1840 - 1893)
arranged by A. Kleinecke

Allegro in tempo di Valse

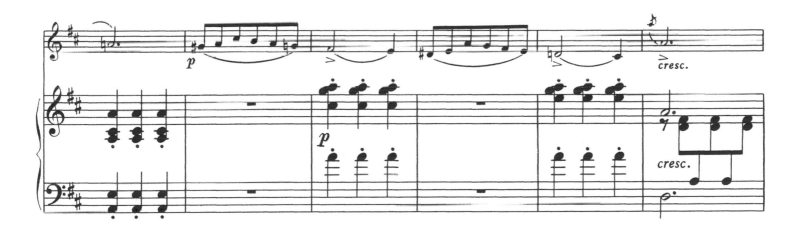

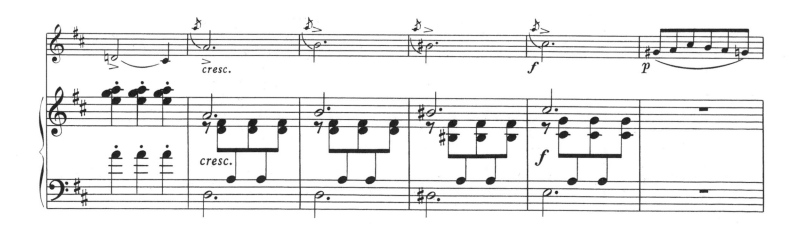

15. Aria

from: Alexander Nevsky

SERGEI PROKOFIEV (1891-1953)
arranged by Josef Gingold